Butterfly Life Cycle

Written by
Laura Appleton-Smith
and Susan Blackaby

Laura Appleton-Smith holds a degree in English from Middlebury College. Laura is a primary school teacher who has combined her talents in creative writing with her experience in early childhood education to create *Books to Remember*. She lives in New Hampshire with her husband, Terry.

Susan Blackaby has worked in educational publishing for over 30 years. In addition to her writing curriculum, she is the author of *Rembrandt's Hat* (Houghton Mifflin, 2002); *Cleopatra: Egypt's Last and Greatest Queen* (Sterling, 2009); *Nest, Nook, and Cranny* (Charlesbridge, 2010), winner of the 2011 Lion and the Unicorn Award for Excellence in North American Poetry; and *Brownie Groundhog and the February Fox* (Sterling, 2011). She lives in Portland, Oregon.

Text copyright © 2013 Laura Appleton-Smith and Susan Blackaby

All Rights Reserved
No part of this book may be reproduced or transmitted in any form or by any means, electronic, mechanical, photocopying, recording, or otherwise, without prior written permission from the publisher.
For information, contact Flyleaf Publishing.

A Book to Remember™
Published by Flyleaf Publishing
Post Office Box 287, Lyme, NH 03768

For orders or information, contact us at **(800) 449-7006**.
Please visit our website at **www.flyleafpublishing.com**

Eighth Edition 2/20
Library of Congress Control Number: 2013957844
Soft cover ISBN-13: 978-1-60541-153-8
Printed and bound in the USA at Worzalla Publishing, Stevens Point, WI.

*For Nicole, my good friend and exceptional assistant.
Thank you for all you do and for being you.*

LAS

To the Red-tailed Readers

SB

The Life Cycle of a Butterfly

A pretty butterfly flying past is quite a sight.

2

But did you know that a butterfly does not start its life with wings?

A butterfly starts its life as a caterpillar. Then it changes. But how?

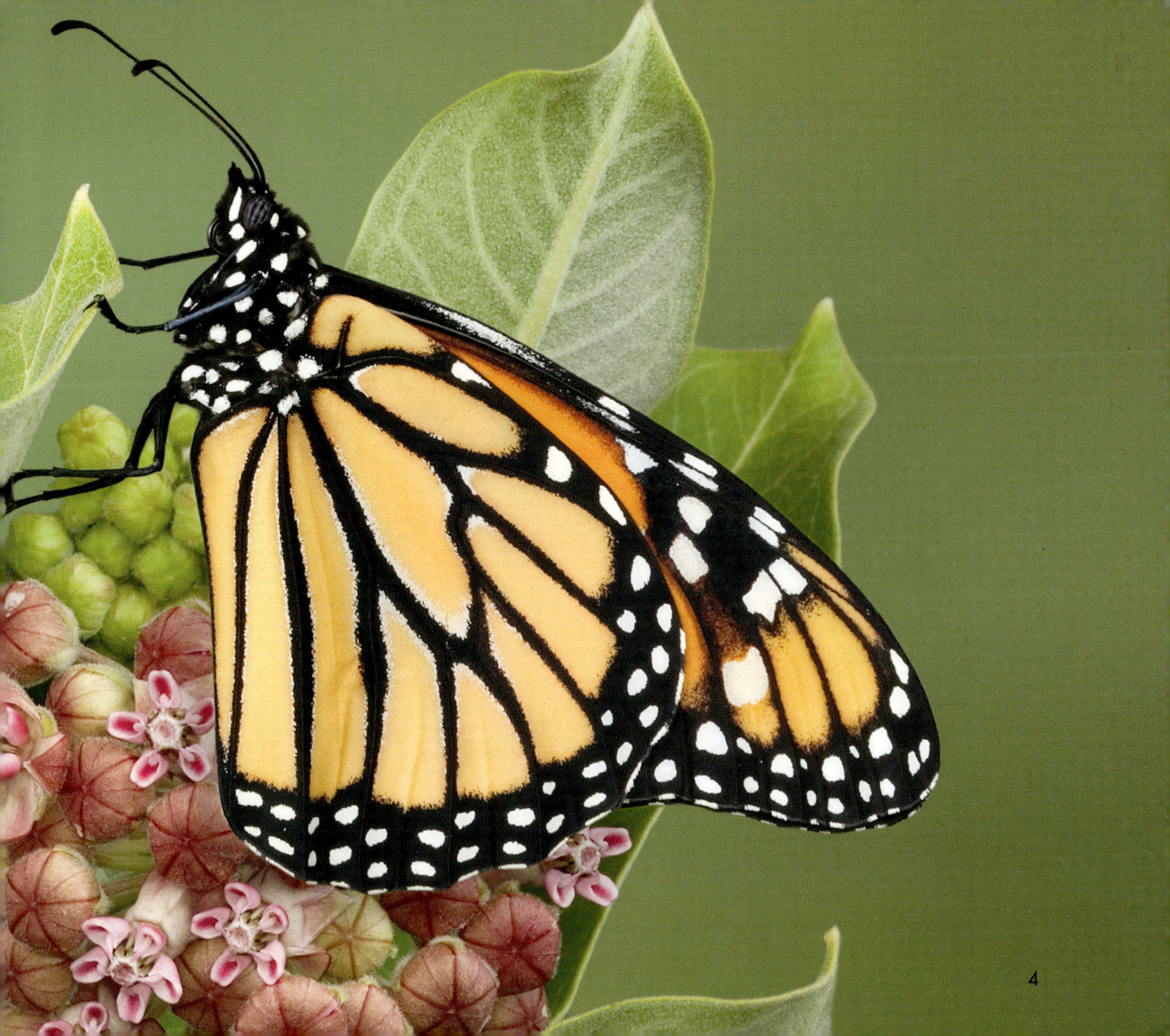

Metamorphosis

During its life, a butterfly changes form, or shape, as it grows. People who know about insects use the word *metamorphosis* when they talk about this change of form.

The metamorphosis of a butterfly has four stages, or steps:

Stage 1: Egg

Stage 2: Larva

Stage 3: Chrysalis

Stage 4: Butterfly

6

Stage 1: Egg

Like other insects, a butterfly lays eggs.

The little butterfly eggs stick to the underside of leaves.

A butterfly can lay more than one hundred eggs at a time!

Most of these eggs do not survive.

Other insects and birds eat many of them.

8

Stage 2: Larva

Within three days to two weeks,
a *larva* will hatch out of each butterfly egg.

A butterfly larva is called a caterpillar.

A caterpillar can be fuzzy. It can have stripes.
It can have spikes and spines!

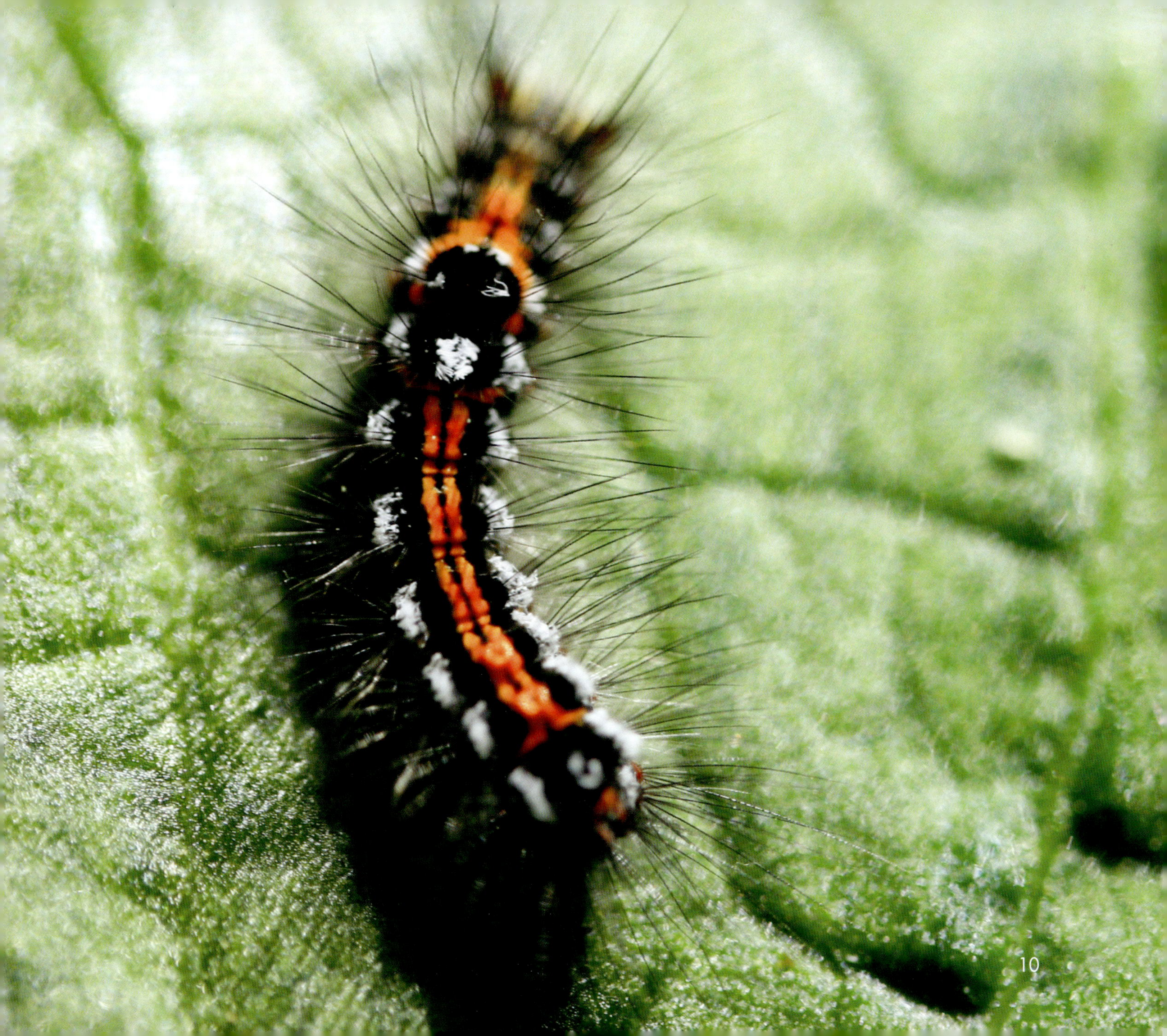

A caterpillar begins its life on the leaf of the plant where it was hatched.

While the caterpillar is too small to go far to get food, it has a supply close by.

The little caterpillar eats the leaves of the plant it hatched on.

The caterpillar spends all its time eating. You can see the bite marks the caterpillar makes on the leaves it eats.

Stage two of the metamorphosis is the growing stage.

The caterpillar sheds its old skin five or six times as it grows bigger and bigger.

After about two weeks, it is time for stage three. It is time to make a change.

New skin

Old skin

Stage 3: Chrysalis

When it is time to change, the caterpillar hangs upside down in a safe spot out of sight.

The caterpillar sheds its last layer of skin and grows a shell. This shell is called a *chrysalis*.

Chrysalis

Inside the chrysalis, the larva changes into an adult insect.

If it is cold outside, this stage might last through the winter. If it is warm outside, this stage might last only a short time.

18

Stage 4: Butterfly

When it is time, the chrysalis cracks and a butterfly creeps from it.

The butterfly sits for a while to let its wings dry. Then it takes flight into the sky!

20

Stage four of the metamorphosis is the flying stage.

The butterfly is an insect that is on the move.
It can travel long distances.
Some kinds of butterflies can fly
hundreds and hundreds of miles.

Butterflies need energy to fly. Most butterflies survive by drinking sweet liquids like nectar or tree sap.

Why does a butterfly fly long distances?

It might need to go to a place
where it is warmer in the winter.
It might need to seek out a mate.
It might need to fly to a safe place to lay its eggs.

24

The Full Cycle

When the butterfly gets to the right place, it will lay its eggs. Then stage one of the metamorphosis begins again.

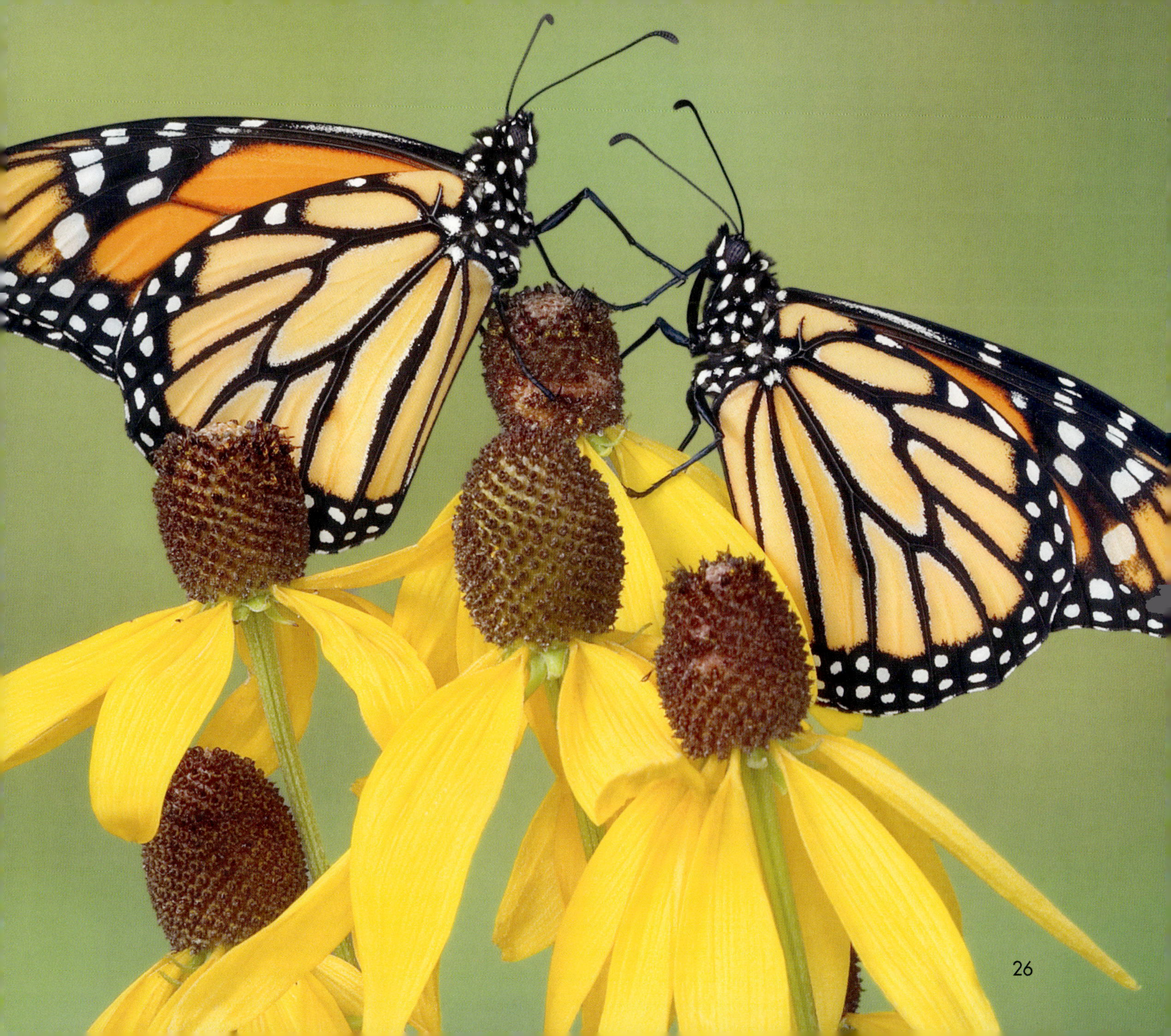

The butterfly life cycle starts over:

Stage 1: Egg

Stage 2: Larva

Stage 3: Chrysalis

Stage 4: Butterfly

Glossary

chrysalis   The outer shell around an insect pupa.

cycle   Steps that repeat over and over in the same order.

larva   A newly hatched insect.

metamorphosis   A change in form that happens in stages.

nectar   A thick, sweet liquid.

stage   A step in the process as something develops or grows.

Story Puzzle Words

begins	leaf
butterflies	leaves
caterpillar	move
chrysalis	nectar
flight	outside
glossary	pupa
lay	repeat
layer	sight
lays	

Decodable Words

1	egg	marks	step
2	eggs	mate	steps
3	energy	metamorphosis	stick
4	far	need	sweet
100	for	not	takes
a	form	on	talk
adult	fuzzy	or	than
after	get	order	that
all	gets	part	the
an	hangs	past	them
and	has	place	then
animal	hatch	plant	these
as	hatched	process	thick
at	hundreds	safe	this
bigger	if	same	three
birds	in	sap	travel
but	insect	see	tree
called	insects	seek	tucked
can	is	sheds	turns
case	it	shell	use
change	its	short	weeks
changes	larva	sits	when
changing	last	six	will
close	let	skin	wings
cracks	liquid	small	winter
creeps	liquids	spends	with
develops	little	stage	within
did	long	stages	word
distances	make	start	world
drinking	makes	starts	

Prerequisite Skills
Single consonants and short vowels
Final double consonants **ff**, **gg**, **ll**, **nn**, **ss**, **tt**, **zz**
Consonant /k/ **ck**
Consonant /j/ **g**, **dge**
Consonant /s/ **c**
/ng/ **n[k]**
Consonant digraphs /ng/ **ng**, /th/ **th**, /hw/ **wh**
Consonant digraphs /ch/ **ch**, **tch**, /sh/ **sh**, /f/ **ph**
Schwa /ə/ **a**, **e**, **i**, **o**, **u**
Long /ā/ **a_e**
Long /ē/ **e_e**, **ee**, **y**
Long /ī/ **i_e**, **igh**
Long /ō/ **o_e**
Long /ū/, /o͞o/ **u_e**
r-Controlled /är/ **ar**
r-Controlled /ôr/ **or**
r-Controlled /ûr/ **er**, **ir**, **ur**, **ear**, **or**, **[w]or**
/ô/ **al**, **all**
/ul/ **le**
/d/ or /t/ **–ed**

Target Letter-Sound Correspondence

Long /ī/ sound spelled **y**

butterfly	flying
by	sky
cycle	supply
dry	why
fly	

Target Letter-Sound Correspondence

Long /ī/ sound spelled **i_e**

bite	spines
five	stripes
inside	survive
life	time
like	times
miles	underside
quite	upside
spikes	while

High-Frequency Puzzle Words

about	many
again	might
also	more
another	most
around	newly
be	of
between	one
cold	only
days	other
do	out
does	outer
down	over
during	people
each	pretty
eat	right
eating	some
eats	they
food	through
from	to
go	too
growing	two
grows	warm
have	warmer
how	was
into	where
kinds	who
know	you